SLINKY SCALY SLITHERY SNAKES

Dorothy Hinshaw Patent

Illustrations by **Kendahl Jan Jubb**

DEVELOPMENTAL
STUDIES CENTER™

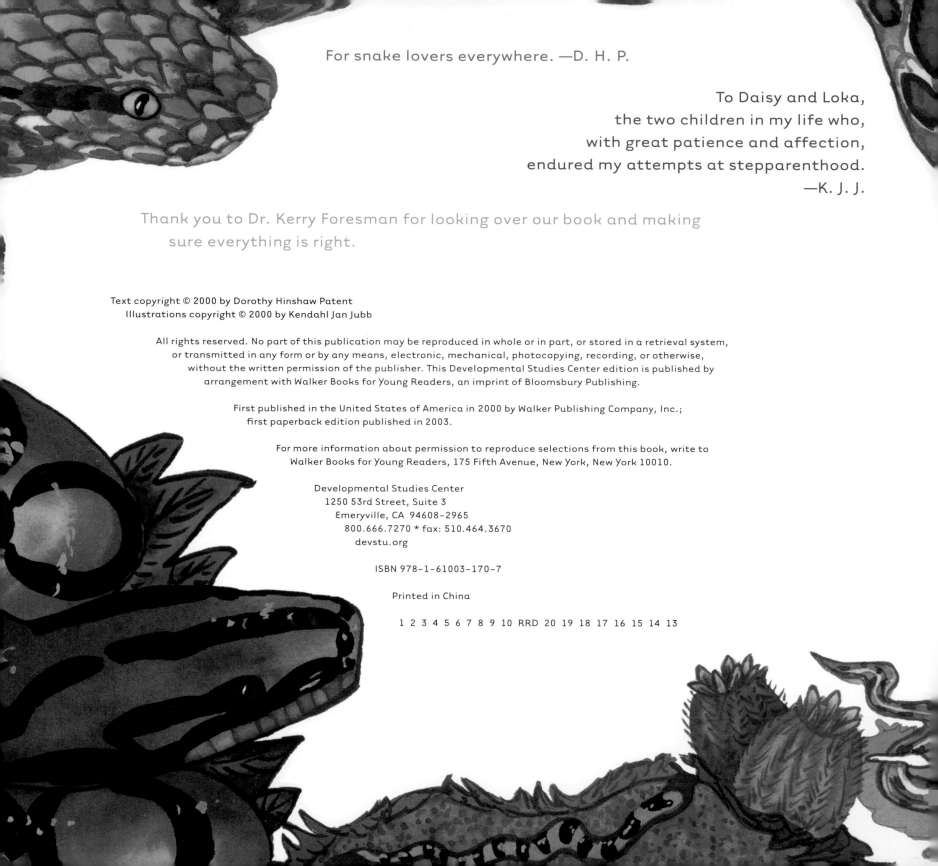

For snake lovers everywhere. —D. H. P.

To Daisy and Loka,
the two children in my life who,
with great patience and affection,
endured my attempts at stepparenthood.
—K. J. J.

Thank you to Dr. Kerry Foresman for looking over our book and making sure everything is right.

First published in the United States of America in 2000 by Walker Publishing Company, Inc.;
first paperback edition published in 2003.

For more information about permission to reproduce selections from this book, write to
Walker Books for Young Readers, 175 Fifth Avenue, New York, New York 10010.

Developmental Studies Center
1250 53rd Street, Suite 3
Emeryville, CA 94608-2965
800.666.7270 * fax: 510.464.3670
devstu.org

ISBN 978-1-61003-170-7

Printed in China

1 2 3 4 5 6 7 8 9 10 RRD 20 19 18 17 16 15 14 13

You'd think it would be hard to survive in the wild without legs. But look at snakes! More than 2,500 kinds slither and creep throughout the world. Snakes live just about everywhere except on some islands and near the North and South Poles. They can climb the tallest trees or burrow deep into the earth. Some snakes never leave the water. Others remain forever on land.

3

Snakes have only one shape, but they come in many different sizes. Two-inch-long thread snakes are as skinny as a strand of spaghetti. But a thirty-two-foot reticulated python is big enough to eat a pig or even a small person.

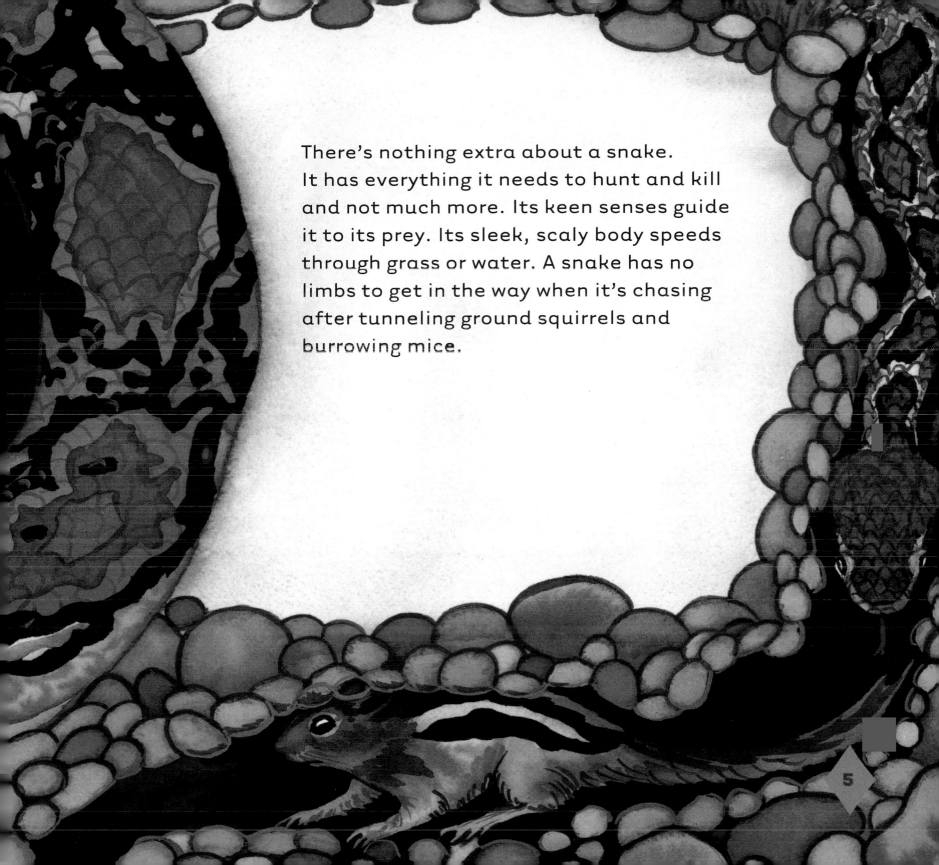

There's nothing extra about a snake. It has everything it needs to hunt and kill and not much more. Its keen senses guide it to its prey. Its sleek, scaly body speeds through grass or water. A snake has no limbs to get in the way when it's chasing after tunneling ground squirrels and burrowing mice.

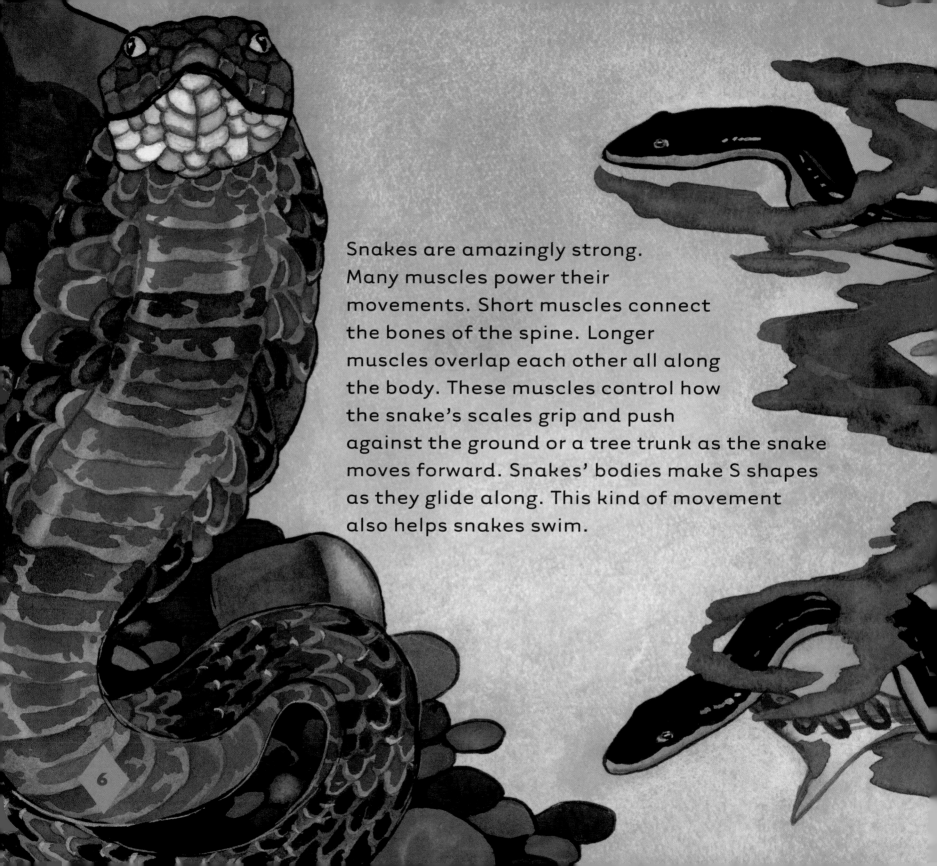

Snakes are amazingly strong.
Many muscles power their
movements. Short muscles connect
the bones of the spine. Longer
muscles overlap each other all along
the body. These muscles control how
the snake's scales grip and push
against the ground or a tree trunk as the snake
moves forward. Snakes' bodies make S shapes
as they glide along. This kind of movement
also helps snakes swim.

6

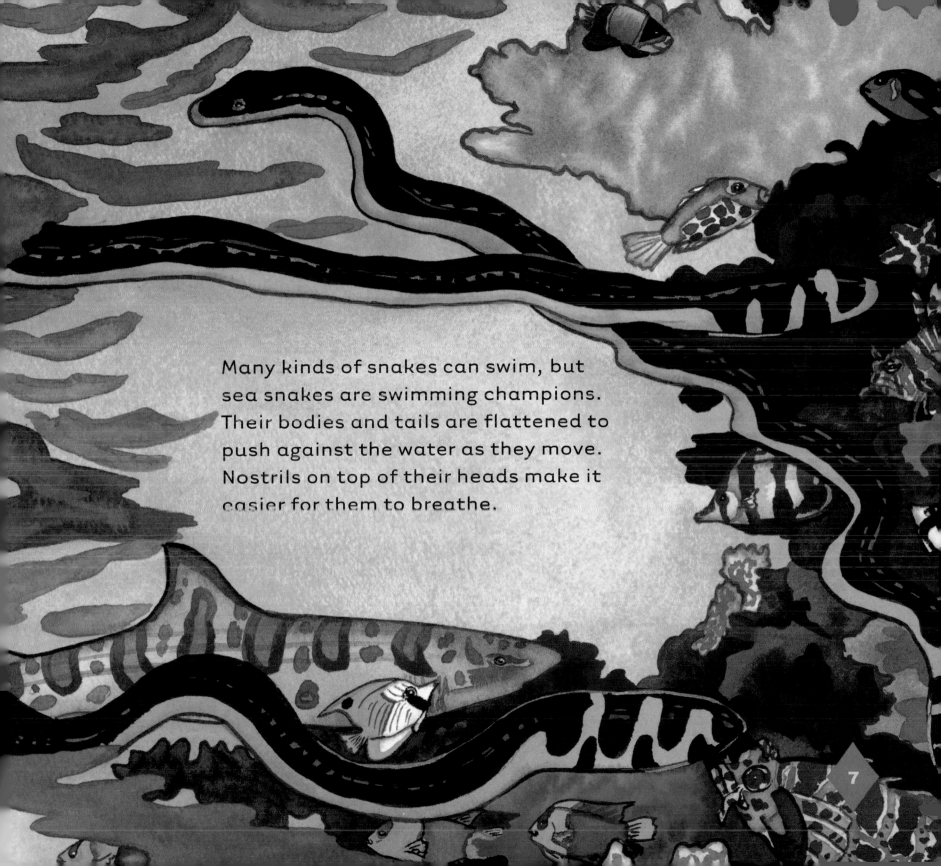

Many kinds of snakes can swim, but sea snakes are swimming champions. Their bodies and tails are flattened to push against the water as they move. Nostrils on top of their heads make it easier for them to breathe.

Some snakes swim through water, but shovel-nosed snakes swim under desert sand to avoid the heat. Sidewinders seem to swim over the surface of the desert, looping their way quickly from place to place.

Trees are a perfect home for many snakes. A long, thin body can wind through the most tangled branches with ease. But moving against gravity can be a problem. Many snakes that live in trees have ridges on the scales of their bellies that cling to the bark of a tree as they climb. Others wind their tails around one branch as they stretch toward the next branch with their heads.

Snakes have many ways to avoid attack by other animals such as eagles, raccoons, or badgers. Snakes may use sound as a warning. Most pit vipers have a tail spine they beat against dry leaves to make a warning sound. Rattlesnakes go one step further. They have a built-in rattle on the ends of their tails. When a rattler feels threatened, it coils its body and raises the tip of its tail, shaking the rattle rapidly. The loud buzzing sound means "Stay away or I'll bite."

A cobra knows how to scare its enemies. Its front ribs are especially long and can fan out to the sides to make a wide hood behind its head.
A cobra raises the front of its body when it spreads its hood. Some cobras hiss or growl, too. The most dangerous cobras don't just threaten, they spit poisonous venom at the eyes of their enemies, then flee.

The teeth of nonpoisonous snakes can't do much damage to a predator, and even the fastest snake has a hard time escaping from an animal with four legs, so some snakes have ways of tricking their enemies. Many have rounded tails that look like their heads. When threatened, these snakes hide their heads and show their tails. The predator attacks the tail, and the snake can wriggle free and escape head first.

The eastern hog-nosed snake is a champion trickster. When threatened, it lifts and flattens its neck, and hisses. If the enemy comes closer, the snake strikes at it with its mouth closed. If that doesn't work, the snake violently twists its body about, vomits, and defecates. Then it rolls over on its back and lies completely still, its tongue hanging from its open mouth as if it were dead. When the enemy leaves, the snake turns over and crawls off.

Many poisonous snakes, such as coral snakes, use their bright markings to warn other animals to stay away.

Some harmless king snakes and milk snakes look enough like poisonous ones that predators leave them alone.

Other snakes use their colors to hide. You can tell how a snake deals with danger by its color pattern. Snakes that slither away often have striped bodies. The stripes make it hard to see that the snake is moving at all, until suddenly it's gone.

Many snakes that live in trees are green. Their color hides them well. Some are also long and thin like vines. People walking in a tropical forest must be careful if they reach for a branch or they might grasp a snake by mistake.

Snakes are camouflage experts. Solid brown or gray snakes lie on the forest floor partly covered by leaves. The leaves break up the snakes' long, thin outlines. Snakes decorated with spots and blotches also blend in with their surroundings, making them hard to see. These patterns are just as good for hiding the snake from its prey as from its predators. Many of these snakes lie in ambush, sometimes for weeks, waiting for their prey to show up.

Some snakes attract their prey instead of ambushing it. The tail tips of such snakes are brightly colored in white, pink, or yellow. The snake holds its tail up and wiggles the tip while the rest of its body is hidden by its dull colors. The curious prey comes close, and the snake grabs it.

A snake's senses help
it find food. Snakes can't
hear well, but they easily feel
vibrations through the ground.
Many snakes have poor eyesight, but
they all have a keen sense of smell, which
is by far the most important way a snake
takes in the world around it. When a snake flicks
out its forked tongue, odor particles from prey or
other snakes that have passed by stick to it.
Sense cells inside the snake's mouth
react to the odor particles and tell
the brain what's out there.

19

Heat-sensitive nerve endings on their heads allow many snakes to feel the body heat of their prey. Pit vipers have these sensors concentrated into two pits that lie between their eyes and their nostrils. Scientists think pit vipers can also tell the shape or size of a warm-blooded animal using these pits.

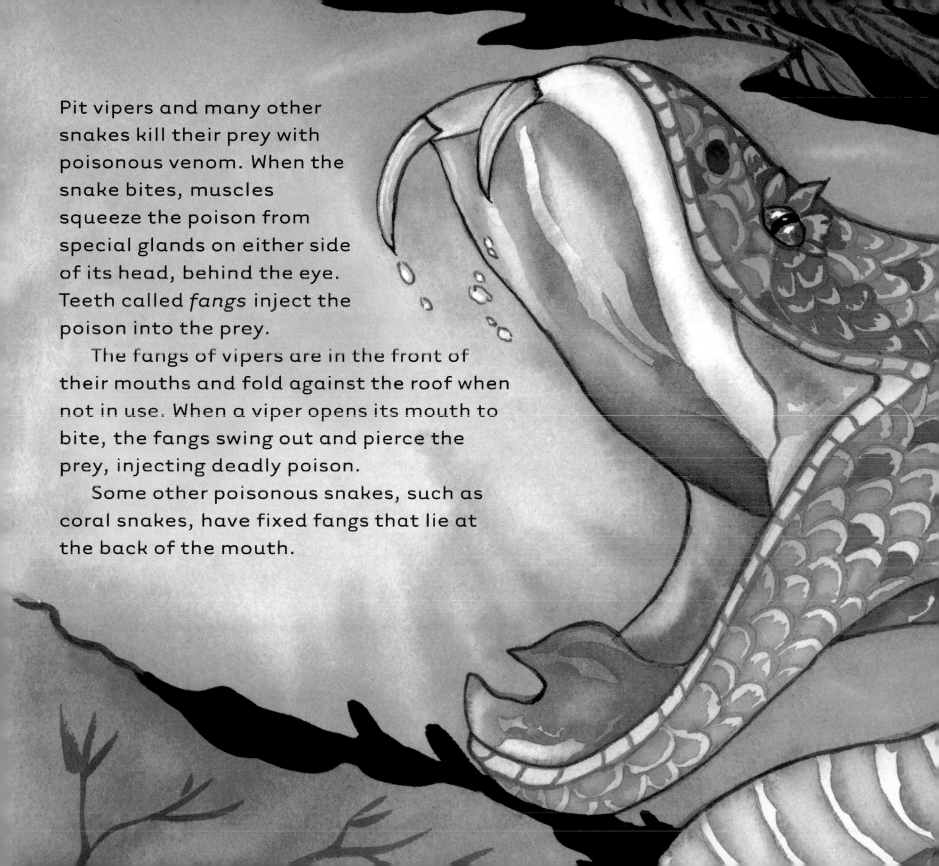

Pit vipers and many other snakes kill their prey with poisonous venom. When the snake bites, muscles squeeze the poison from special glands on either side of its head, behind the eye. Teeth called *fangs* inject the poison into the prey.

The fangs of vipers are in the front of their mouths and fold against the roof when not in use. When a viper opens its mouth to bite, the fangs swing out and pierce the prey, injecting deadly poison.

Some other poisonous snakes, such as coral snakes, have fixed fangs that lie at the back of the mouth.

The blunt-headed vine snake uses its strong body to sneak up on lizards. A lizard naps on the tips of ferns so that an approaching snake will shake the plant and wake the lizard. But these tree snakes have a secret weapon.
They can hold their slender bodies straight out into the air. A hungry blunt-headed vine snake can climb a neighboring plant, stretch its body over, and grab the sleeping lizard.

Pythons and boas are called *constrictors*. Their bite isn't poisonous. They kill instead by wrapping themselves around their prey and squeezing it so it can't breathe and its blood can't flow. Soon, the prey is dead. Then the snake releases its hold and swallows the food whole.

How does a long, slender animal eat something bigger in diameter than itself? A snake's lower jaw bones can swing down and out around the body of its prey. By moving first one side of the upper jaw and then the other forward, the snake "walks" its mouth over the food until it enters the snake's throat and can be swallowed.

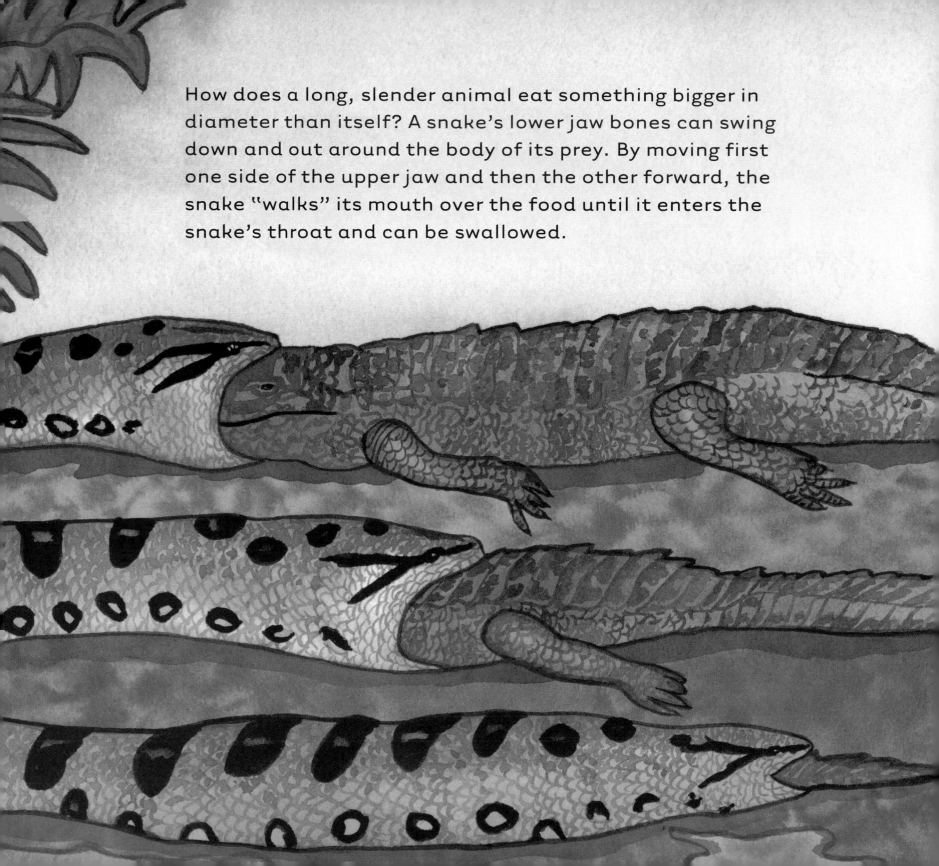

"Eat seldom, eat big" is the motto of most snakes. Warm-blooded animals like birds and mammals use some of the calories they get from food to keep their bodies at a constant warm temperature. Cold-blooded animals such as snakes don't do this. Their body temperature varies with the surrounding air temperature. Cold-blooded animals need only about a tenth as much food as mammals of the same weight. A snake might only need to feed three or four times a year if it finds large prey. After a big meal, a snake may lie in the sun to warm its body and digest the meal faster.

In cold climates, some snakes, like garter snakes, spend the winter together in dens. When it warms up in the spring, the snakes mate before separating.

In other species, male snakes find the path used by a female and follow her trail. If two males find the same female, they fight to see who is stronger. This battle is called a combat dance.

Most snakes lay eggs. The shell of a snake's egg is tough and leathery, not hard like a bird's egg. The female snake lays her eggs in the ground or in the nest of another animal. The mud snake looks for an alligator's nest and lays her eggs there. When the female alligator protects her own eggs from predators, she ends up protecting the mud snake's eggs, too.

Some mother snakes take care of the eggs they lay. The female king cobra uses her body to pile plant material into a nest in a bamboo thicket. Then she lays twenty or more eggs in the nest and stays with them until they hatch.

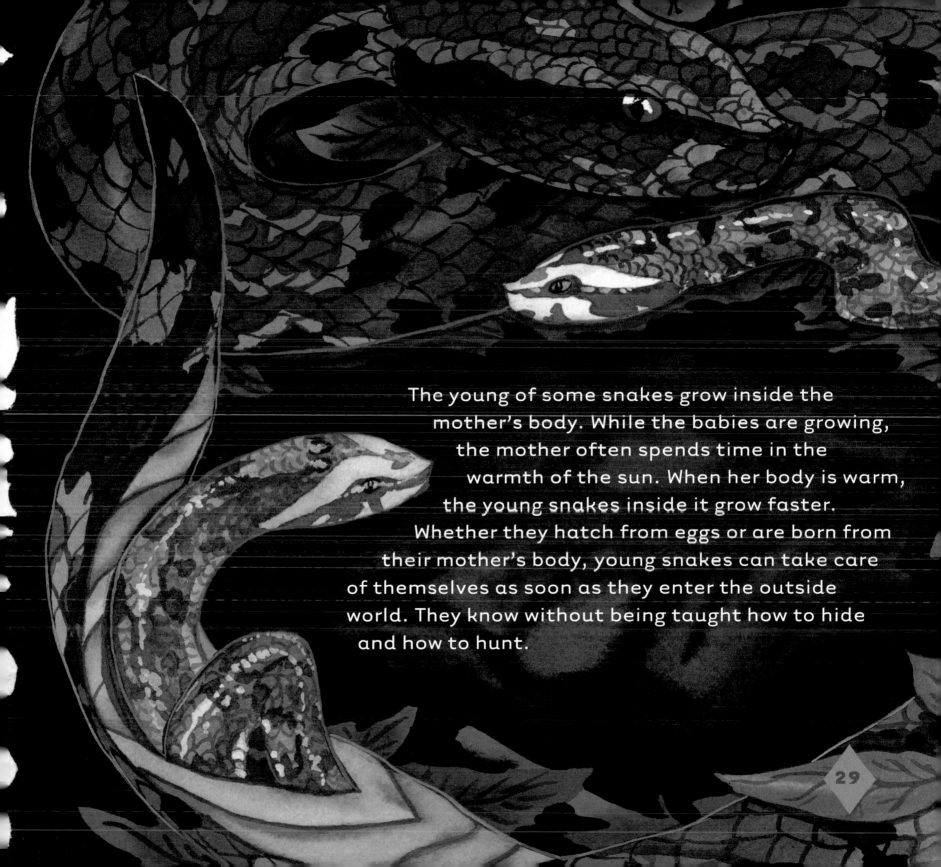

The young of some snakes grow inside the mother's body. While the babies are growing, the mother often spends time in the warmth of the sun. When her body is warm, the young snakes inside it grow faster. Whether they hatch from eggs or are born from their mother's body, young snakes can take care of themselves as soon as they enter the outside world. They know without being taught how to hide and how to hunt.

When snakes are brought to new places where they don't belong, they can cause trouble. The brown tree snake normally lives in New Guinea and northern Australia. But in the 1940s, it "hitchhiked" on board ships to the island of Guam. Guam had no native snakes. The birds there had no way of defending themselves against the brown tree snake. By the 1980s, Guam swarmed with snakes but few forest birds remained on the island. The snakes had eaten them. Fruit bats and lizards were also disappearing fast. People are trying to get rid of the snakes, but it isn't easy.

Many kinds of snakes that were once common are now rare. When forests are cut down, the snakes that live in them lose their homes. New highways, shopping malls, and private houses also destroy the homes of snakes.

Some people don't like snakes. They don't understand that most snakes are harmless to people and can actually be helpful to humans by eating rats, mice, and other pests. Snakes themselves are also food for other wild animals. It's important to realize that all animals, including snakes, have a place in nature.

SCIENTIFIC NAMES
(in order of appearance)